Pottery

By Heather Hammonds

T0342769

Contents

How Pottery Is Made

Pottery is made of clay that has been baked until it is hard and strong.

Bowls, cups, plates and pots can all be made of pottery.

Pottery has been made for thousands of years.

pottery from ancient Greece

A potter makes pottery.
First, the potter takes some wet clay
and makes it into a shape.

A potter can make pottery
on a potter's wheel.
The potter's wheel spins round and round.

a potter's wheel

After pottery has been made, it is left to dry.
Then it is baked in a kiln,
so it becomes hard and strong.
A kiln is a very hot oven.

a pottery kiln

Pottery that has been baked
is then painted with special paint.
The paint is called glaze.

After pottery has been painted with glaze,
it is baked in a kiln again.
The clay becomes harder.
The glaze melts and becomes shiny.

Pottery must cool down slowly
after it has been baked in a hot kiln.
Then it will not crack.

Some potters make pottery
so they can give it to friends and family.

Some potters sell their pottery
to earn money.

Many people like to buy pottery.

Make a Coil Pot

Goal

To make a coil pot.

Materials

You will need:

- special modelling clay from a craft shop
- a plastic board
- a plastic knife
- a baking tray
- an oven, heated to 110 degrees Celsius
- an adult to help you.

Steps

1. Push and roll the clay in your hands, until it is smooth.

2. Cut the clay into equal pieces.

3. Roll the pieces into long coils on a plastic board.

4. Wind one coil round and round in a spiral shape to make the bottom of the pot.

5. Press the edges of the coil together gently with your fingers, until it is smooth.

6. Add another coil to the bottom of the pot to make the sides of the pot.

7. Wind more coils onto the pot to make it taller.

8. Press the sides of the pot together
with your fingers, until they are smooth.

9. Put the pot on a baking tray.

10. Ask an adult to bake the pot
in the oven for 30 minutes.

11. Ask the adult to take the pot out of the oven after it has finished baking.

12. Wait for the pot to cool, before you use it.